God Is So Good

Cindy Tubbs

ISBN 978-1-0980-7768-6 (paperback)
ISBN 978-1-63844-774-0 (hardcover)
ISBN 978-1-0980-7769-3 (digital)

Christian Faith Publishing, Inc.
832 Park Avenue
Meadville, PA 16335
www.christianfaithpublishing.com

Printed in the United States of America

To Kiki, my grandson

Kiki is four years old and is autistic. I have the privilege of driving him to his therapy school during the week. On the way to school, he seems to enjoy my storytelling. Kiki is currently nonverbal, but we pray God will show his mercy and grace and give Kiki his words.

Our Lord loves Kiki—we are sure of that! So we are trusting in that love and will allow God to work in our lives through this situation and give him praise through it all.

For we know that in all things

God works toward the good

of those who love Him and are

called according to His purpose.

—Romans 8:28

Today is a rainy day!

Where did the sunshine go?

The sun must be hiding behind the clouds.

Where does the rain come from?

Well, God makes the rain!

He holds the rain in the clouds and

then lets it come down on us.

He makes it rain so that the trees

and the grass and the flowers

will have water to grow.

Rain also gives the animals water to drink.

Animals, big and small, need water to drink.

Like elephants (they sure are big).

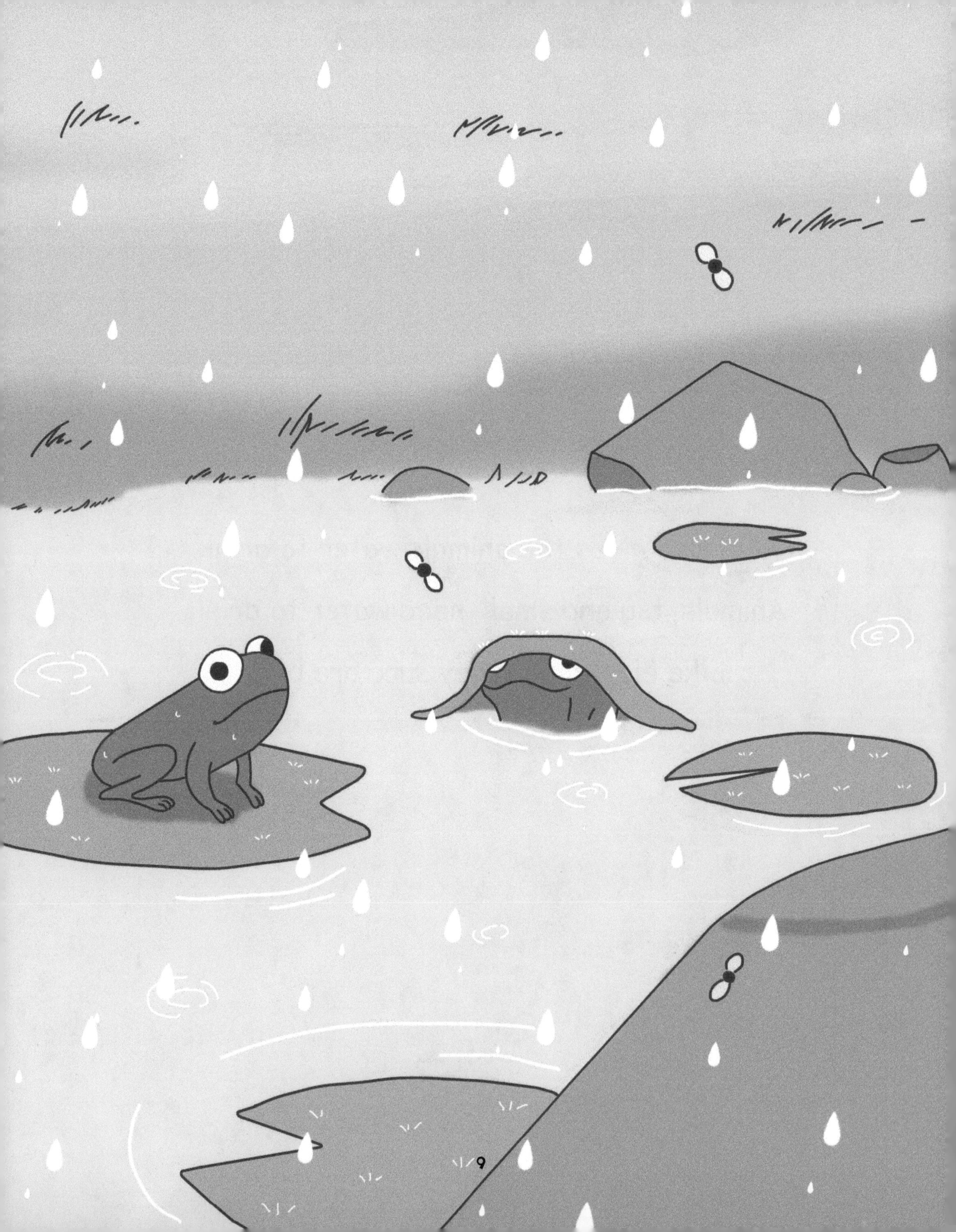

And frogs (they sure are small).

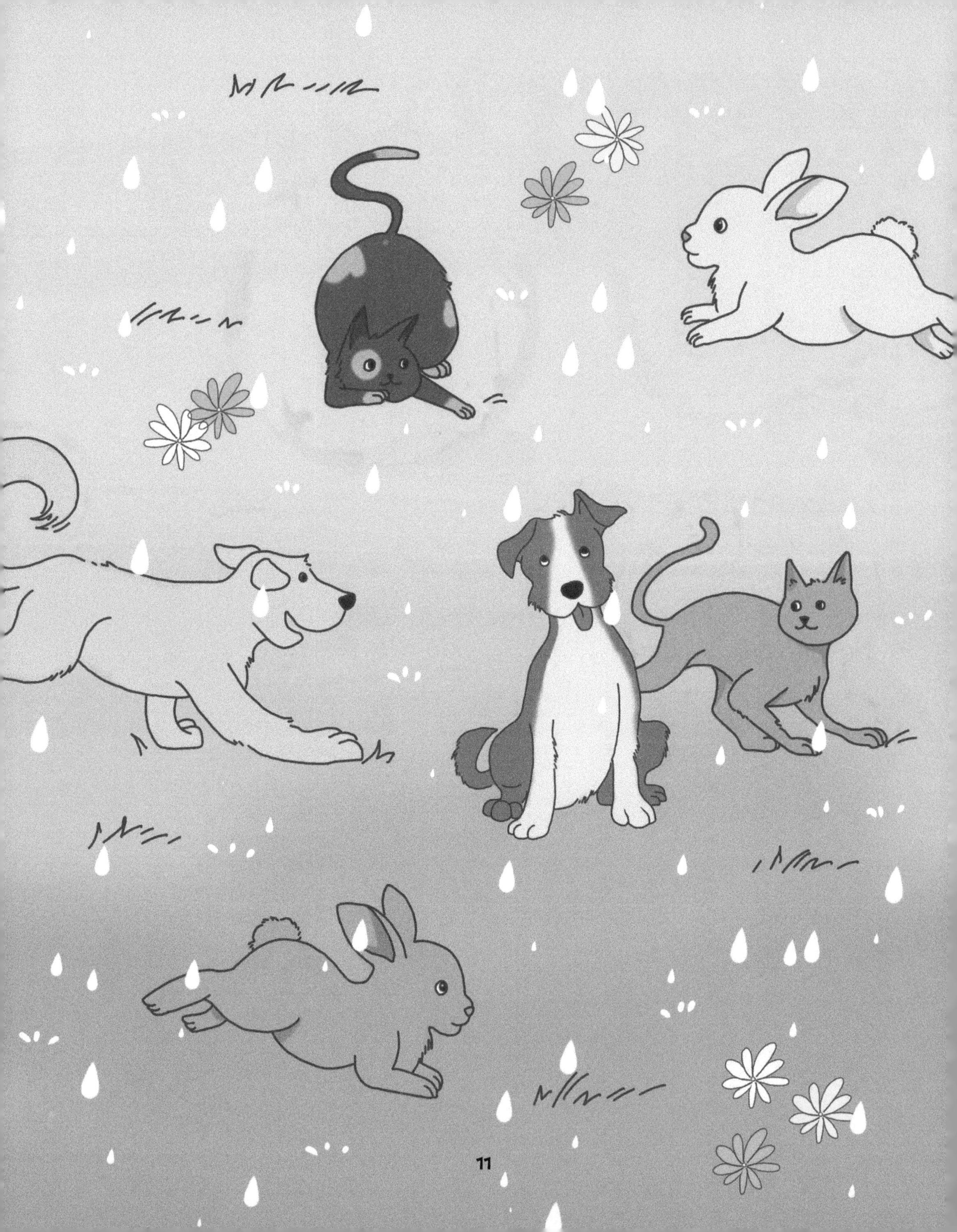

And rabbits and cats and dogs and even

the birds that fly need water to drink!

(Birds even like to take a bath in the rain.)

And ducks (they sure like the rain!).

We also need the rainwater.

Rain gives us water to drink—

and water for a bath!

(I like to take baths!)

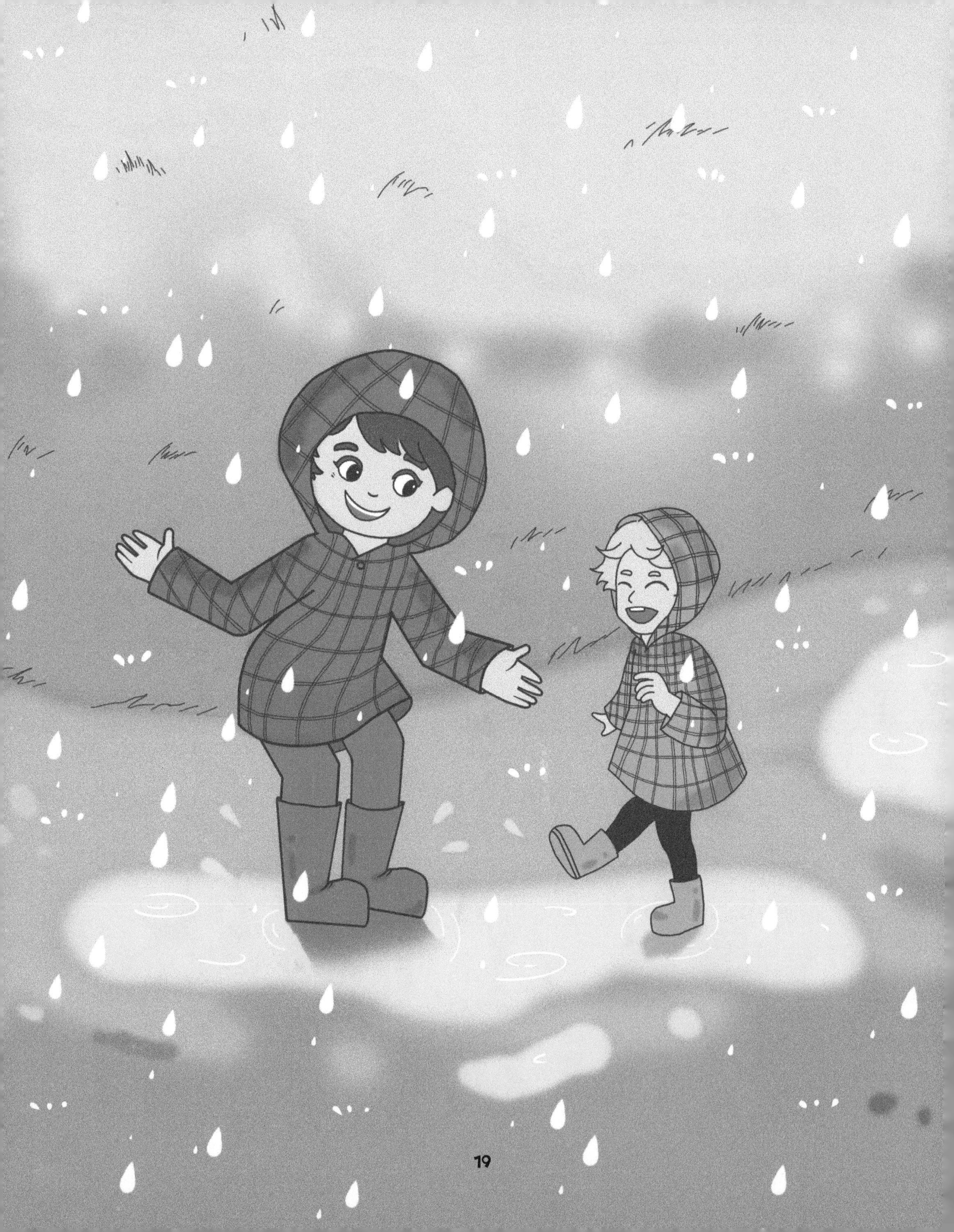

God waters me! Sometimes,

on a warm rainy day, my mommy lets me and

my little brother go out to play in the rain!

Rain can make mud puddles.

I like the mud puddles!

With our rubber boots on, my brother Ian and

I can splash in the puddles and even

run through them!

Sometimes, after the rain is over,

the sun peeps out from behind the clouds,

and there could be a rainbow in the sky!

Rainbows are so beautiful.

Rainbows have beautiful colors in them:

pink and blue and purple and green.

God gives us the rainbow as a

promise that he will always bring

the sunshine back after a rain.

Do you like the rain?

Thank you, God, for *rain*!

Our God is So Good!

About the Author

Cindy and her husband John have been married for 49 years and they have two sons; John II, who is married to Sandy; and Michael, who is married to Lisa.

Her five grandchildren are Katie, Jacob, Noah, Kingston (Kiki), and Ian. Her love of family is surpassed only by her love for her Lord Jesus Christ.

Being active in church is a priority and a blessing for her. She is devoted to expressing her faith and love for her Savior to her family, her grandchildren, and to lost people.

Her greatest desire is for people to see Jesus in her.

CPSIA information can be obtained
at www.ICGtesting.com
Printed in the USA
BVHW021403200721
612416BV00005B/874